Poetry OF THE Spirit

BOOK 2

Inspirational thoughts that explore our
Divine Nature and the beauty of our universe

JOE ALFIERI

BALBOA.PRESS
A DIVISION OF HAY HOUSE

Balboa Press books may be ordered through booksellers or by contacting:

Balboa Press
A Division of Hay House
1663 Liberty Drive
Bloomington, IN 47403
www.balboapress.com
844-682-1282

Because of the dynamic nature of the Internet, any web addresses or links contained in this book may have changed since publication and may no longer be valid. The views expressed in this work are solely those of the author and do not necessarily reflect the views of the publisher, and the publisher hereby disclaims any responsibility for them.

The author of this book does not dispense medical advice or prescribe the use of any technique as a form of treatment for physical, emotional, or medical problems without the advice of a physician, either directly or indirectly. The intent of the author is only to offer information of a general nature to help you in your quest for emotional and spiritual well-being. In the event you use any of the information in this book for yourself, which is your constitutional right, the author and the publisher assume no responsibility for your actions.

Any people depicted in stock imagery provided by Getty Images are models, and such images are being used for illustrative purposes only. Certain stock imagery © Getty Images.

Print information available on the last page.

ISBN: 978-1-9822-5250-2 (sc)
ISBN: 978-1-9822-5251-9 (e)

Balboa Press rev. date: 08/24/2020

CONTENTS

Acknowledgements ix

Preface xi

Dedication.. xiii

The Flame.. 1

Winds of Light... 2

Energy... 3

Gratitude 4

Flow of Life 5

Candles 6

Consciousness.. 7

Celebrate Life... 9

Feelings Of Love.. 10

Forerunners.. 11

Essence of Christmas... 12

Corridor of Light.. 13

Eyes to See 14

Live Life Fully 15

Life's Blessings 16

Empathy and Compassion 17

Sunbeams 18

Essence 19

Morning Dove 20

Vibration 21

Resurrection 22

One Source 23

Purification 24

Vocation 25

Normandy 26

Essence of Love 27

Quest for Love 28

Special Graces 30

Inner Child 31

Fruit of the Master 32

Scent of Heaven 33

Droplets of Love 34

No Ordinary Moments 35

Self Mastery 36

Enlightenment 37

Reconnection 38

Beyond The Scope 39

Behold God 40

Free Will 41

Soulmates 42

Realization 44

"Simple Truths" 45

Afterword 49

ACKNOWLEDGEMENTS

With much Love and Gratitude to my special children; Dear daughters Carin, Sandra and Shari for the gifts they bring to the world in the areas of Art, Compassionate Service and Spiritual Teaching.

To my dear wife Sharon who has always allowed me the space, with Love, to scribe these verses.

To Dee Wallace a super teacher who more than gently nudged me to publish Book 2.

A special thanks to Grandson Ryan for providing his much needed technical expertise.

This edition also includes a special section titled "Simple Truths." They are thought provoking nuggets, which over the years have been shared by a variety of Inspired Teachers. Do hope you will enjoy their philosophic bent.

PREFACE

The problem is forgetting who we are. Thus the real journey in this world is to discover our true Identity. We often forget, that we are in fact all pieces of God; made in his image and likeness.
These poems are silent keys to help us remember our birthing Graces.

DEDICATION

This Book is dedicated to the Creator of everything we see, feel and experience and to the Spiritual Teachers in every dimension who have guided my life and my writings.

THE FLAME

Each year of Spiritual exploration
continues to reveal truths
that have been dormant
within the dimensions of soul

from this special place
we eventually come to fully realize
our Divine connection with all things
as we are guided through
avenues of splendor
within the ethereal flow

and then, as if by magic, in the Silence
we eventually behold ourselves
as hearts-afire
with the flame of love

it is here the actual Light of our Heart,
"The Divine Presence" appears to us
as a thousand Blazing Suns
which we can call upon
to overcome all illusions.

WINDS OF LIGHT

What were these swirls
that returned my breath
to feelings and sounds of joy

they were winds of light
wiping out the cobwebs
of illusionary despair

and so this light now parades
throughout my being
as a never-ending reservoir
of love

ready to absorb any encounters
that attempt to move my center
away from Source.

ENERGY

Energy is the mortar of life itself
gifted to all creation
and it moves and dances with every atom
to the music beat of each heart

the power of its force
flows about as malleable substance
and like clay is shaped and molded
in images we cast before us

what songs will each of us send forth
with melodies that excite our soul
to channel this wondrous energy
along pathways that fulfill our goals

why not choose rhapsodies of purple velvet
with the radiant splendor of Saturn
and in this illumined scenario bring to fruition
the high energy dreams we have patterned.

GRATITUDE

Whatever vicissitudes in life may come your way
it is important to take time at the close of each day
to recall special moments and blessings we've known
which have graced us with a glimpse of heaven's own

recalling these feelings from deep memory
are a cleansing jewel for this journey
as they remove and wash away much old debris
they will reset our sails with new purpose and glee

our changing views of earthly dualities
most assuredly point us toward harmonious shores
for they fill us with loving forgiveness and grateful
hearts
which return us to vistas of glory.

FLOW OF LIFE

All goodness flows to every heart
whose door is open wide
it brings enormous peace and joy
much like a rushing tide

so be of good cheer, knowing that
the flow will come your way
when you are one in spirit
with the Life Force, day by day.

CANDLES

When lighting candles
to commemorate a person or solemn event
we are inwardly showered
with moments of joy
as these dancing candle flames
graciously remind us
of love's manifold blessings.

CONSCIOUSNESS

That eternal something
traversing the universe
found in every particle of substance
is none other than, Divine Consciousness

in sand and rocks and grass and trees
in flowers and food and bushes and leaves
in worms and critters and animals and US
is found pure strains of consciousness

it varies by degrees of course
in terms of utilizing the source
but it is ever present in all we see
a subtle part of cosmic energy

each displays the code within its core
revealing it for what it is, and nothing more
in mankind however has been placed the key
which can when focused set us free
tis "the power of creative thought"

it may be used to scale those lofty heights
of blissful purpose and kingly flights
to that place where the circle of light is shown
allowing each to choose it, for their very own

through meditation and by grace
one may take residence in this hallowed place
for all have been gifted to move beyond earth's realm
and by tapping pristine levels propelled by thought
we may tread the paths great Masters before, have
walked

this lifting of self above matters core
to that Third Tier, of God's holy sphere
will uncover the shining Star within us
and move our light-filled souls into Super
Consciousness.

CELEBRATE LIFE

Rejoice all ye of vintage age
play all the flutes
ring all the bells
it has been an amazing trip

we've climbed the mountains
won the races
shared our goodness
with many faces

so celebrate these memories
with Joy and Love
knowing the best you had
did indeed, touch many hearts.

FEELINGS OF LOVE

Let us highlight some sacred moments
of love in full display;

when we are filled with inner joy in appreciation
of the arts—
when we are moved by the blissful sounds of music—
when we are flooded by a panorama of nature's
wonders—
when we share our warm affection and kindness
with
family, friends and teachers—
and when our heartfelt passions of devotion and
gratitude are bestowed upon our beloveds—

the unseen magical ESSENCE of these precious
experiences
meld us into feelings of radiant Oneness
and lift us into new realms of peace and serenity.

these "Love Feelings", provide a full measure of
cherished moments, and nudge us to silently
embrace
the marvelous vision of Camelot.

FORERUNNERS

We are all individual explorers
probing the inner dimensions of consciousness
and each step we take
moves us to new levels of awareness

much gratitude is due
those early forerunners
who with sustained courage,
often at personal risk
removed the chaff
from well-trodden paths of thought

their efforts have lifted everyone
to new and higher levels
of vibrating reality

now each of us are challenged
to continue this progression
by offering our special gifts
to an ever-evolving society.

ESSENCE OF CHRISTMAS

This winter wonderland of Christmas
always evokes wondrous feelings
of excitement, gratitude and awe
as colorful lights, decorative tree ornaments
and the aroma of freshly-cut pine
transport us into dream-like realms
of youthful joy and expectation

all this, coupled with the magical feeling
of Inner Peace on this holy day
remind us that we too, are of Divine Origin
lovingly linked in a Union of Oneness
with all humankind

these precious reflections
of nostalgia, love and sacred identity
become for each of us
the uniquely special, Essence of Christmas.

CORRIDOR OF LIGHT

We are always in,
God's corridor of light
but it is only as wide or as narrow
as the space allowed by our mind's eye

so it is important we build an awareness
that expands this highway of light
which can provide much needed guidance
in our journey to greater heights

this process is an inward one
requiring vigilance and control
to keep thoughts in an uplifted mode
in all our daily roles

truly the magic resides
in soul's unceasing desire
to reach levels that pave the way
for a widening of this holy path
in our contemplations day by day.

EYES TO SEE

Countless miracles of nature surround us
in every shape and size
and in reflective moments
manifest their beauty before our eyes

need we continue to ask
the cause behind such precious science
whose show of love brings forth royal majesty
in every stroke of nature's brush

these eternal rhythms confirm a benevolent creative
force
sustaining each of nature's molds
which lavishly displays its elegance throughout the
universe
for every creature to gratefully behold.

LIVE LIFE FULLY

Live life to the fullest
treasure each hour, each day
for time will not return to you
once it has passed this way

live life with humor and fun
enjoying all the wonders of earth
and remember to thank the maker of all
for each precious moment, since birth.

LIFE'S BLESSINGS

Count all your blessings in life
without trying to number each one
just know, that the goodness that happens your way
is governed by thoughts, you select every day

as you choose the wisdom, of this original thinking
readily available for all to employ
a marvelous life, will move within your grasp
filled with numberless blessings and joy.

EMPATHY AND COMPASSION

In life's daily encounters
the empathy of friends, help bring to light
the innate joy within ourselves
often hidden from our sight

to have special friends with gentle smiles
and eyes that speak in precious ways
do buoy our spirits at those times
when burdens seem to mask our days

such valued moments, shared in common air
fill our hearts with a sense of peace and victory
and produce a depth of hope and understanding
over whatever our problems may be

what a blessing it is to receive support
during these periods of trouble and strife
for they help forge needed moments of courage
as we travel the pathways of life.

SUNBEAMS

We are all manifestations
of Divine Energy
and we express ourselves
through the color
of the frequencies we project
these variations blend into one
to comprise the magnificence
of an evolving creation

it is here, free will allows us
to choose those Sunbeams
that will shape our Sacred Journey
as we seek to merge with
the Eternal Source of Love.

ESSENCE

One can always sense that unique essence
in special journeys through life
when we are moved
by a spark of magnificence
that ignite in us, a radiant light

each experience a sublime encounter
that leaves us never the same
whether they are
energetic portraits of special people
or of nature's ethereal plains

when one is touched by such essence
pure joy surges within the heart
and then seemingly
our whole world changes
and becomes ablaze with loving light.

MORNING DOVE

We first heard your beautiful tones
many years ago at our lovely cottage
just 4 houses from Lake Erie

and how refreshing it has been these many years
to awaken each morning
to your melodic cooing

even with our gypsy wanderings
you journeyed along and continued
your peaceful morning renditions
that helped us set the rhythm for each day

now in these later years
when moves are no longer required
you still daily bless us
with your joyous sounds

so thank you, Dear Morning Dove
for these many moments of peacefulness
and the continuing feelings of serenity
that you generate with your soothing tones.

VIBRATION

The basic substance of all creation
surrounds every living thing
and can be molded and shaped, into whatever we
desire
as we attune our minds, from within

no special key is required
to materialize the pictures we hold
just an abiding belief, that the power of thought
will give birth to all the images, brought forth

the frequency of your mind generates vibes
which produce all conceivable patterns
that bring to fruition the seeds we have planted
in glorious manifestation

therefore, elevate your thoughts and feelings
through positive affirmations
realizing the Divine Self within
will actualize their creation
there is no secret in this method
ordained when life began
simply raise your vibrational level
and gather to you, the wealth of heaven.

RESURRECTION

Arise in consciousness
and lift your-Self, above the mortal veil
partake in heaven's wonderous bliss
and so proclaim, that a son of God, prevails.

ONE SOURCE

Oh glorious Father
the source of all power and light
I thank you for all thy gifts
which have made my life, so bright!

PURIFICATION

Continual release of an negative patterns
affecting those we touch
will bring the cleansing elixir
that we desire so much

this step will lead us upward
a new world we will enter
for then we will discover
we are a Power Center.

VOCATION

Enjoy your role in life
whatever it may be
for it is filled with hidden treasures
far beyond what can be seen.

NORMANDY

These shores which appear so peaceful and majestic
were once blurred with the haunting fears of young
patriots
who strung themselves upon the sands with selfless
abandon
knowing not if this would be,
their private Armageddon

the debt is great and can never be repaid
except to honor such devotion
with deeds that shout in an ear-bursting chorus,
beyond those cliffs
that we solemnly commit each of our generations
to freedom's cause, come what may.

ESSENCE OF LOVE

Love is an unconditional force
that emanates from within the heart
flourishing as flowers in Spring
with each act of kindness we impart

contrarily, inward expressions of displeasure
subtlety created over time
color our world with invisible barriers
which deny us a loving life

know then, each simple act of caring devotion
will move us toward that bright arena
where joy and peace will fill our souls
with the promise of loving achievement.

QUEST FOR LOVE

My family experiences, revealed the magical
relationship of marriage
and convinced me, that if one could find a partner
to share this worldly trip, of challenges, achievements,
disappointments and joys
then life's segment would be fulfilled.

It all began, in early life
the search for one, to be my wife
in school I'd often, screen the field
hoping love's promise, would be revealed

But none I found, did meet the test
of life long's measure, for happiness
and so with dreams, holding love's mystery
I ventured forth, to serve my country

While in duty, I searched throughout the land
from shore to shore, and in distant clans
but nary a one, could find a place
into my heart's, treasured space
So upon my return, to freedom's land
still searching for, that precious hand
I placed my fate, in God and good
knowing, I would not be misunderstood

And then one day, from the distant blue
I caught a glimpse, of that one so true
and instantly knew, that it was she
the girl that fate, had led to me

We courted, for a little while
and then I asked her, with a smile
will you be mine, on this trip through life
she nodded yes, I'll be your wife

The message of these words exclaim—
When one seeks love, with abiding faith
it will surely come, if we but wait.

And now, some fifty years are here
filled with memories nothing can eclipse
with love sustained through life's many tests
it has truly been a wondrous trip.

SPECIAL GRACES

The great I AM
continually whispers to me
awaken, to the limitless power of your Special Graces
which are innate in all of us

the original message of the ethereal reminds us
that while humanity was created
in the image and likeness of Source
also <u>Silently</u> included
were ALL of the Creator's Special Graces

so now, a new Spiritual Renaissance is upon us
ushering in a grand and mighty shift in Consciousness
and calling us to fully exercise the Gifts of our True
Identity

there are no limitations in this heavenly arena
where the overflowing radiation of Divine Light
hearkens us, to access these Special Graces
as beloved heirs of the Kingdom.

INNER CHILD

In the Spring of Youth
we follow life's path with the faith of a child
and as the seasons change
that precious embryo faces many new challenges
on how to walk or run or weave our way
through earthly cobwebs of adversity

these winds of change are designed to move us
to fresh horizons of growth and understanding
and a new arena of consciousness
where we can begin to experience
the many mansions resident in each of us

so with resolve,
let us move into contemplative meditation
calling upon the wisdom of the Inner Child
to bring our Energy Fields
into greater dimensions of Light and Love
where they can be touched
by the supreme knowingness and tranquility
of the higher spheres.

FRUIT OF THE MASTER

Let all who would send messages
extolling thy blissful aroma of peace,
love and harmony
graciously display in the outer
that which they inwardly profess

there is no greater voice of spirituality
which we are blest to witness
than this evidential quality
of the illumined self.

SCENT OF HEAVEN

Throughout life
there is a yearning
to move ourselves into
touches of Spiritual Light

it is a zone
where fears melt
and no challenges
are too great

the Quest is finally realized
when we discover
this heavenly realm
is simply our Inner Room
where it is filled with
the Scent of Love's Aroma.

DROPLETS OF LOVE

*Our heartfelt thoughts of the past
remind us of the many special souls we've known
and the wondrous times we've shared
while probing the beauty of God's creations*

*oftentimes, we ponder these joys with Unwept
"Tears"
for they remind us of the emotional energy of Divine
Love
and cause us to reflect on those endearing words
penned by dear friend, Jan Price*

*so with simplicity and reverence let us revel
on this special portrait of words.*

"Tears are Droplets of Love"

*(I recall Jan's husband, John Price
saying, this simple phrase certainly
deserves Framing)*

NO ORDINARY MOMENTS

There are no ordinary moments
as Dan Millman, has proclaimed in his scroll
each allow us to fashion, special patterns of mind
which can lift and caress the soul

be assured, they are spiritual carriers
for whatever thoughts you may wish to convey
and these moments become, what each of us make
of them
by our actions day by day

so choose wisely the path of your feelings
charge each moment with the power from above
and it will respond to your inner essence
with inspiration, confidence and love

there are no ordinary moments
each are filled with the challenges of life
which all lead to personal growth and fulfillment
when viewed, in a positive light.

SELF MASTERY

While our early years may seem difficult and
perplexing
because we subscribe to resentment and worrisome
moods
we eventually learn to correct this thinking
by gaining a proper perspective of truth

thus, as we face future challenges and trials
we realize the choices we make are our own
then it is clear we can alter "the effects of cause"
thereby changing the seeds we have sown

How can this be done you say, once the seeds begin
to grow?
When the master law has been set in motion, what
can change its flow?
If we return to our higher nature with understanding
and heart-filled love
this will move us into the next dimension obviating
the laws from above.

ENLIGHTENMENT

Reveal thyself to me, Father
let me behold thy face
as the reflection of every living form
which permeates all space

ignite that deeper yearning
which rests within my soul
let it bring forth enlightenment
and thus fulfill, my lifelong goal

let me sense thy awesome splendor
surround me with thy precious light
then, lift me into oneness with you
where eternal bliss and goodness reside.

RECONNECTION

Eternal frequencies of God
you fill this earthly sphere
with boundless streams of energy
across each evolving tier

so let all who seek to interact with
these light-filled healing springs
move steadfastly toward "The Reconnection"
knowing, this noble quest will be fulfilled.

BEYOND THE SCOPE

The spacious wonders, manifest before us
limitless, in human terms
yet so apparent for all to see
the glories, within our galaxy

such detail and precise movement
in all of nature's rhythms
reveal God's auric hand, all about
far beyond the scope, of human doubt.

BEHOLD GOD

I rejoice each time I sense the essence of your Presence
as reflected in every atom of nature's domain
in the trees, the flowers, all plant and animal life
but most assuredly, in the Divineness of human life

so as we daily travel the arena of this living universe
*let us **often** call to mind these two mystical words*
in recognition of, that Divine Oneness
embedded in all life forms.

BEHOLD GOD!

FREE WILL

Every day is a gift
inscribe on it what you will
and so underscore heaven's assurance
of promises to be fulfilled

countless choices to be made
as we walk our path in life
experiencing the joy of free will
while trusting soul to guide us aright.

SOULMATES

Marriages are made in heaven, as the adage goes
and are scripted with poetic beauty
projecting visions of growth and harmony
which foretell its voyage upon the earthly sphere

once the pact is sealed, fated souls parade among
the clouds
lying in wait until that magic moment
when they are beamed to common destinations
to begin their joint drama of redemption

there are no coincidences, in this most serious of
life's choices
for each converging soul has chosen this holy alliance
and needs only the vibrant color of the other
to bring forth brilliance, and fulfill itself

but in the run of our experiences
some may find what appear to be, insurmountable
problems
when in fact, they are simply the special challenges
set forth
before the, beam was cast.

What time is taken, to reflect on such pre-earthly covenants?
How true are we, to early vows of love and glory?
Or do these heavenly pledges barely cross our minds
as we are subordinated to mundane cares!

Has the original karmic jewel somehow escaped our grasp
and left us, in a morass of exterior entanglements?
If so, then our grand storehouse of virtues must be resurrected
to sustain the early forging, of this divine partnership
which was designed to share a wondrous trip!

As we awaken the light within our hearts
to love's enduring theme of compassion and selfless devotion
it will elevate us to those higher planes of understanding
with recollection, of the great adventure promised.

Soulmates can then indeed, continue a glorious journey, as no other,
on their inexorable course toward enlightenment
heeding the vision of their commitment as they trod
life's measured miles, in search of the eternal quest.

REALIZATION

While our daily challenges
may at times, cause us concern
through intuitive exploration
we are able to unearth
a variety of appropriate solutions
from within our Sacred Center

and so, with Heartfelt Love
the innate gift of this Inner Wisdom
does allow us to tap into all the Graces
we will ever need to access
both for ourselves, or to share with others

So Rejoice!!!
Knowing, it is within our province
to visualize and call forth
a streaming bond of light-filled energy
to realize our journey into wholeness.

"SIMPLE TRUTHS"

1. *Those who bring sunshine to the lives of others cannot keep it from themselves.*

2. *In reference to problems we encounter, reflect on this; an oyster takes an irritation and makes of it a magnificent pearl. How many pearls can we make in a lifetime?*

3. *It doesn't matter what school you attend, the right Teacher will always be there.*

4. *We sometimes think only the visible world has reality—but think of the many things which we cannot see and yet do exist e.g. thoughts, feelings, imagination, electricity, gravity, radio frequencies, magnetism, wind, cold, heat, air, sound, odor, energy, Love.*

5. *With all the books on Philosophy, Psychology and Sociology it's amazing that the solution to all personal conflicts is simply to "Treat others as you wish to be treated".*

6. *Give up your personal history. Leave your old garments behind and healing opportunities will present themselves.*

7. Regarding criticism directed toward you—if you do not accept the gift, to whom does the gift belong?

8. Always remember to trace the rainbow in the rain.

9. Everything we have is loaned to us for only a season.

10. Truth is like a jewel, it has both beauty and lasting value.

11. Love is only for the young, the middle-aged and the old.

12. There are two lasting things we can give our children; one is roots and the other is wings.

13. Do not let anyone color within the lines of your life's mission.

14. Gratitude is akin to the most awesome sunsets and sunrises.

15. The sun is always shining behind the clouds.

16. To enjoy the flavor of life; take big bites.

17. When love and skill come together, expect a masterpiece.

18. What a new face courage puts on anything.

19. Help me to understand the truth about my self— no matter how beautiful it is!

20. *One cannot seek to find truth and be unattended.*

21. *The love in your heart wasn't put there to stay—*
    love isn't love until you give it away.

22. *True prayer is not begging and pleading but a*
    heartfelt desire filled with love.

AFTERWORD

*Sitting before us in plain view are the most important words ever recorded; they are in Genesis 1-27—which says, "We are made in the Image and Likeness of our Creator". This means that at birth we were all created as pieces of God which contain the Father's Essence, His Light and His Energy. How wonderful is that! This anchored I AM Presence in each of us has been described by Ascended Masters as The Sacred Heart which is located in a Holy Chamber near our normal heart area. We can enter this Holy Chamber at any time by simply Stilling ourselves for a few moments and desiring to be in Communion with the Father, **who is always there**. We can also visit this Sacred Chamber as often as we like—**for it is within us**. It is truly a powerhouse of Spiritual Energy which we can call upon to help us meet any of life's challenges. We know that a simple prayer filled with Love is all that is required even though the Father also knows our needs. It is however truly a joy to mentally visit this special area and to feel and experience the Presence of our Creator.*

A Tribute

Painted by
Uncle John Alfieri

Printed in the United States
By Bookmasters